THE
SIGNATURE
OF THE
S P I R A L

THE
SIGNATURE
OF THE
SPIRAL

DANIEL WELLS SCHRECK

Sunstone Press
Santa Fe, New Mexico

First Edition

Printed in the United States of America

Library of Congress Cataloging in Publication Data:

Schreck, Daniel Wells, 1953-
    The signature of the spiral / Daniel Wells Schreck. – 1st ed.
    p.   cm.
    ISBN 0-86534-114-1 :
    1. Southwestern States–Poetry. I. Title.
PS3569.C52917S5   1989
811'.54–dc19   87-16469
                                                                    CIP

Published in 1989 by SUNSTONE PRESS
                Post Office Box 2321
                Santa Fe, NM 87504-2321 / USA

For Ethel Burnham Wells

CONTENTS

Tsi Mayoh (*for* Alfonso Ortiz)

Breath of life!
Navel of the world
Thank you for saying,
"We return to the spot we started from."

Mesas amber
Pinon studded
Sangre de Cristo cool
Jemez warm

And the river of our valley
The grey fox haunt
Running trout thick
I listen

I listen to thunder rumble
I watch the rain clouds mass
I hear you breathe
I see without seeing

I feel the day grow long
The cloak of night cover me
Back to the lake from whence we came
Back to the spot we started from

Vision Bread (*for Michael Ortega and Randy Rice*)

In Chimayo–
    we bit off a piece of vision,
    like fry bread,
    our mouths streaming,
    we chewed on the host.
Each day–
    we bent our backs over the land,
    three green acres of cottonwood paradise,
    cool shade sheltered us from the heat,
    while the river murmured,
    and the red mesas,
    etched in ribbed pastel,
    guarded the shrines of the ancestors.
In the late afternoon–
    we watched medicine bundle clouds sprinkle
    first offerings of pollen blessings and ripe berries
    onto sacred bosom spots where hummingbirds gathered,
    the rain pouring full into thirsty open lips.
The sun–
    never forgot to incite us,
    in light layers of vision over the clouds
    that as we worked to plant our seeds,
    rainbows arced double over the mesa.

At dusk–
    the mountains lit up in auric fire
    our efforts were rewarded
    by feeling,
    our spirits close to us
    breathing,
    leaving loaves of bread with us
    baking,
    the flame of vision accomplished,
    burning.

Magpies

The magpies flying above my field
and landing on the fence post squawking
are people I knew in high school. The ones
in letter-sweaters and cheerleader skirts
who were always popular, black and white stripes,
their pride and glory.

My cat gazes at them knowing they are untouchable.
Yet he click-clacks in his throat,
animal adrenalin tasting them.

Big birds spend their time stealing flower seeds
from the soil when the farmer has forgotten
to plunge his planting stick down far enough
in the field to escape probing beaks.

The magpies' place in the sun is assured.
They proclaim it to each other through the day.
If my cat and I tire of them it's because
in being left out, we have learned patience,
and now watch our seeds sprout in their time.

The Meeting

Ah, Mercedes!
Nice to meet you.
What are you doing?
I called about the herbs.

The pot you're cooking on the stove
smells pretty good.
I dip my finger in.
Caramba!
Es picante,
muy deliciosa.

She watches my movements,
a cat, monitoring me,
the flash of a dream appears.

The full moon hangs fat in the night.
I am playing with a big black cat.
He is chewing on my hand,
his teeth clasped over the fatty part of my palm.
I calm my fear-he leaves no blood marks.

The kitchen is lit up with light.
I see her smiling at me,
the sun moving from behind a cloud,
bursting in upon us.

I think it occurred to both of us that day,
in the hours towards twilight,
on my lap her big black cat nestling,
how have we come to be together?

We sit with our arms locking,
rocking on her back porch swing.
In a shiny purple the mountains are bathed.
Fire bleeds into the clouds over the Jemez.

Feeling and thoughts just come to the surface.
We know that this love takes it cue
from the spirit,
me and the cat,
she and the shaft
of sunlight living,
breaking colors
behind the clouds.

Your Cool Green Eyes

I met you on a day,
it seemed like any other,
your cool green eyes were kind.

The sun's candle flickered,
the flame burning lingered,
lighting blossoms in your dark brown hair.

In the evening glow
I recognized
someone I had not known before.
You were the woman from many dreams.

When you smiled
it wasn't the first time,
a memory of your kindness
like a blazing ring around the moon.

Will your tenderness keep me safe?
May I plant flower seeds
in the holy dirt of the shrine
the earth goddess sculpted in your honor?

Your cool green eyes answer
all the questions
I ever had about
loving you.

The Summer Mother

The Great Spirit lit a cigarette,
a reed filled with a native tobacco,
fire from a quartz stone.

In January, we smoked a pipe of light
praising the Indian summer days
while basking in earthglow.

Deep within the pulses of the blood
memories of the Goddess reminded us
the summer mother was still to be born.
She covered our eyes with silken handkerchiefs
hiding the land behind her veil,
masking the sun's sweet heat.

She came out wearing her best white dress.
Her legs were long and gangly,
a filly trying to stand.
The membrane peeling from her body
bared a skin of snowfall.

Her body was so soft and damp
and touching her flesh
I felt such a pure, clean, cold,
like the inside of stars
where the fire never reaches.

I make my prayers to the four directions,
fling snow in imitation of her kisses
my fingers spreading fleeing crystals,
condensed starflakes composed
to the harmony of her heart.

The white corn will grow tall this year.
The ears will contain all their kernels.
The name of the corn,
she whispers,
when young girls dance
at their coming-out party for the mother.

We saw the sun again,
a white silhouette kissing the lips of the clouds.
The skies gently closed their eyes.
There is no greater pleasure than feeling
one's feet walk softly on the supine snow.

Pojoaque Pugilists

At the arena in the Indian pueblo of Pojoaque
men of the three races pay admission
to see lady wrestlers challenge all comers
for the price of greenbacks to lay down
and tussle a little bit differently.

I stand on a bench, balancing, to see the spectacle.
A Tewa, in braids smiling, stares too.
A tribal policeman enters and scans faces.
The announcer sing-songs like an auctioneer,
and the men go up to fifty bucks
for the privilege of entering the ring.

The women who parade about are like Haystack Calhoun,
the Sheik, or the Blue Bomber, except that, their version
of stacked is some silicon, while they're led into
a harem of men screaming lustily, like a title fight,
at blonde bombshells busting out of their bathing suits.

The oil pit is greased.
The defending champion poses as if at the beach,
while her manager licks his chops, his hands rubbing
yellow Man-Tan oil between her breasts, all eyes watching
his fingers approach her G-string by way of her tin-pan stomach.

The lucky guy's body is smeared, too, by contact.
They maneuver for position, a pin difficult
as skin becomes slippery, headlocks with the legs
accomplishing only to raise the level of vicarious pleasure
each man imagining himself in similar predicament.

They roll and roll, twist and slide.
Combatants are cheered until the roof rafters rumble.
The battle of the sexes proceeds in gladitorial spotlight.
Beer bottles pop. Grins leer in imagined liaison.
A sweltering fire burns madly through the house.

The lady champion, Gypsy, tells her manager
her hang nail is hurting her. He shrugs,
his snout twitching. She diffidently tells him,
"yes, but you don't know what a tragedy it really is."
She has the crowd's sympathy.

The spread sheets of love have been stained
with viscous oil that is hard to take off.
We have forgotten to feel momentary dread
when a cockroach steals across clean bed covers.
American men have allowed their locks to be shorn.

It was billed as a night of women wrestling all comers.
It was, actually, a night of boxing and bloody noses.

Blinded By the Shine (*for Jim Magnuson*)

New Mexico High Times Banner Headline:
PICURIS PUEBLO BEATS ACID-COWBOYS IN EPIC SOFTBALL GAME
AFTER NO WINS EVER IN SEVENTEEN YEAR HISTORY OF SERIES.
You're standing on the edge of a mountain field,
and the Sangre de Cristo's,
white like virgin down,
are framed against the eastern sky.
The air is just a little bit cold,
but heating up as the sun warms things.

You're talking to the Ojo Sarco boys,
we met a few of them at the lumber mill that day,
remembering, from across the valley, we heard the saw buzzing.
They're chewing Copenhagen and drinking Corona.
They trust you now.
They see no harm in a writer doing interviews
about their lives for an article in Esquire Magazine.
They might even think it was poetic justice,
they're kind of amused.
Why not?

The teams are assembling on the baseball field.
The Picuris Pueblo men, slight next to beefy cowboys.
The Indian women are dark-haired and opal-eyed.
The wives and girlfriends of the Acid-Cowboys
icy blue-eyed blondes.

You're talking to everybody,
extending your hand for a shake,
"I'm a novelist researching New Mexico."
Maybe they'd even make you an umpire,
but maybe you'd decline.
You couldn't see all the nuances of the game,
especially expressions on the faces of the people,
the way the ascending light animates their features,
the types of flowers in the grass,
the cottontails the old Indian men chew between their teeth,
the color of the blankets their women sit on,
the blue-green pine trees, like feathers, in a cap behind,
rising up the low hills and falling down the valleys,
of a northern New Mexico that always lingers in your mind.

And you hear at that moment
a strain from a song, "Goodbye Money Mountain,"
by your friend Michael Martin Murphey,
"When a man sees colors in a muddy creek,
a few specks of gold dust in a sandy stream,
will stake a claim on your wildest dreams,
and I was blinded by the shine,"
but in a good way,
not because of gold fever like in the song,
but because your eyes are getting sun-bleached
by that dry clean light washing your mind.

I'm remembering our conversation
on the drive up here,
about
becoming an outsider.
"It ain't no easy business.
You could lose your way
at any number of points."
"Like?"
"Well, first, of course,
you got to get outside,
the reality frame you're in,
withstand the peer pressure,
Then, there's the psychological, inventory.

And you still got the reentry into society process,
getting your vision into practical application,
in some sort of chosen craft,
without impeding the social progress
you're trying to attain."
You pull over and write it all down,
I assume as character background.
"Stasis sets in if nobody does it.
Things only move forward if someone isn't
buying into the old belief patterns."

We're watching former counter-culture bandidos integrate.
They're playing biesbol, norte-America's favorito.
Jim says, "I think this could maybe make a novel."
And the Indians are the ultimate insider-outsiders
who have to balance not only their own knowledge,
that intimate relationship with the nature spirits,
but a whole new world
of people for whom it hasn't quite dawned on
that the whole world is alive
the rocks,
trees,
The water,
everything.

How do you tell someone who doesn't know?
I guess you have to let them discover it for themselves,
maybe hint at it,
try and lead the way if they ask.
But when will they ask?
When the air is too foul to breathe,
when they've made enough money off nature,
when the water gets too sick to drink.
How much patience do you need?
A shitload.

And now you notice the Indians are winning.
They're nickel and diming the Acid-Cowboys to death
with "Everybody gets a hit,"
"No going for the fence,"
"Bunt,"
"Steal,"
hustling the bases,
the runs piling up,
until it's all tied.

A runner at third is off
at the crack of the bat,
a infield grounder deep
between shortstop and second.
Shorty throws to the plate.

In the rundown,
the Picuris player is staying ahead of the catcher
until he tosses a quick flip to the third baseman.
The runner turns on his heels as if they'd grown wings,
dodges past the catcher before the third baseman's throw back,
and scores the winning run.

Everyone on the team is throwing up their arms, jubilant.
You're laughing,
and everyone is laughing now,
even the losers.
It's funny how ironic it all is,
and you're "blinded by the shine."

Santuario

Luminarias,
Sparks from the furnace,
line the driveways and porches,
love of the saviour pious and humble,
calling for the return.

The sun is again tied to the hitching post,
una piedra intihuatana*,
no shadow cast,
the light captured,
the loop woven.

Pine trees lit with white candles
radiate beside every hearth,
angels' wings fluttering with the jingle of bells,
the bright star surmounted atop the tree,
a sign in the sky.

Bonfires burning,
hands kept warm,
feet tromping in the snow,
send up a plume of red coals,
billowing and shining alongside the stars.

The scent of pinon wafting from the fireplace
warms the fibers of the space between,
currents darting,
the frequency of love
taut as a bowstring.

An invisible hand waves the sensor, invoking,
thin glittering silver strands rustle,
a jingling in his ears,
against the sound of breasts beating,
the pulse of earth,
a thudding drum.

Human voices,
aided by angels,
sing and chant their melody of praise,
and song,
like a prayer,
has no will.

For the child,
the delight of Christmas,
has been born again,
joy and light impregnated,
life rejuvenated until spring.

In every village,
a Bethlehem,
a donkey bearing the human parents,
with three easterners,
schooled in augury,
reading the signs.

Carols praise His arrival.
A manger keeps Him warm.
The animals bask attentively,
as the three wise men offer gifts.
A greater gift awaits them.

In little towns everywhere,
the snow and stars affirm,
in every heart, a Santuario,

a place protected where He can come,
a holy of holies in His image,
resembling us.

*the tying stone

El Mundo

Low Rider low
Marijuana high
"You got some?"
Let's cruise
She's purring
Look at those jeans
Muy guapa
Let's cruise

Out into the mountains
Up past Truchas
Out into the snow
Let's sit in the car

It'll be fun
Listening to the radio
Having another beer
While we murmur

The sound of the tires on the street
Rolling down the hill back to town
Sets the tone of the world passing by
Painting El Mundo on her soul

The Sons of Satan

Dear Lord,

I wish You could help Chimayo. Thieves bedevil the land. They steal from their own families to fill their veins and noses with Satan's powder. They no longer see the beauty of Your creations. Their families weep because such a violation hurts so much and no one has the courage to tesitify against them. I wish we could turn their needles into fountain pens. I wish they could be poets instead of addicts.

These fools are fair-weather fowl. They have it so easy compared to the denizens of New York. They have lost you, Lord. They think Your grace spits blood from the end of a syringe.

The heroin dealer is the black magician. He has zombified these young men, not for betraying the secrets of the Voodoo elders, of how the spirits are approached by ones worthy, but to enhance his own power because he hates You. It is the wrong kind of second death. The soul separated from the body through a mock burial is not turned back towards the good, but kept captive to serve evil.

They think You exist in drugs. As the black magician provides them with these false elixirs, he actually sucks their souls' blood through psychic vampirism. As their master consumes their souls, do these cohorts of the Satanic cult deliver up their boody, while Satan's lieutenant roasts them over the spit of their desire.

Satan's disciple lives in a double-wide trailer. His stereo, t.v., VCR, and waxed automobile are only the best. His stooges sleep in their cars, hungover from their last fix. These truly are the living dead. Luminous fireballs no longer appear in Chimayo. The hounds of hell nip at their heels because they are afraid of You.

Their fear is temporary black vapour Satan has sent. Like Job, decent people have done nothing evil. Elihu is wrong again. You test Your faithful. Satan is but the blind rush when heroin floods the soul.

I have made a cross in the altar of my heart and adorned it with a wreath of roses.

Beware, thieves, the real thorns!

They offer life to anyone who spills his own blood for love and the sins of others who have lost the way.

Oh, Lord, what are we afraid of?

Certainly not these poor shades lingering over the fires of hell trying to keep warm over a cold, cold fire.

We must form again the societies for retying souls to their bodies, and cure them.

This is our spiritual responsibility.

We are all Your native children.

May we take a lesson from our elders and ask your help. Then may we see luminous souls flying again amongst us, reminding us that Your lodestar still attracts our best and brightest.

Amen.

Requiem for the Termite People *(after Andre Schwartz-Bart)*

The dear dross of life has put its stamp on my lonely heart.
To watch the cycle of creation and destruction
requires an infinite patience.
Has all history been like this?
The mindlessness of Empire,
traditional peoples losing their lands,
their sacred shrines desecrated by usurpers.

Does God have a plan in all this?
The Just Men must still live,
one for every generation in every culture in the world,
because the world has not yet ended,
The Creator has not withdrawn
the life forces from earth
for purification.

But, even so,
rivers are burning
The monsters of the underworld have been let loose,
and thunder gods watch them warily
as America's uranium appetite barely wavers.

A county afraid of death waits for its own barbarians
to remind itself it is alive.
Cavafy's Vandals and Visigoths have not arrived,
the Soviet Union is too far away.

Our barbarians strike from within.
They are the termite people who would eat
The forests and the land until
there is nothing left.

To lessen such a holocaust,
which would claim the life of the Last of the Just,
an unknown, by divine will,
mandates the sprinkling of a substance on the ground
that would repel the termites.
For this,
the ashes of termite bones would turn the trick,
ashes milled by their own hands.

The Nature of Fascism

Gaze into this smoking mirror!
The razor sharp edges of light are dulled.
They no longer slit through the hard jelly of the eyeball,
Where rayed scissors cut out white paper dolls.
These forms are now as ephemeral as shade.
Wraiths parade about in our bodies.
They commit crimes and blame them on the foul fiend.

When the wick of the heart has burned down,
Smoke fills the room.

A man appears in the mirror.
He holds a burning candle in his hand.
"Let me light again the blackened ember of your heart," he says.
Flames smolder on the wrong side of the screen.
The world is somehow colder.
Funeral pyres blaze against the onslaught
of death's forbidding chill.
Death is a cold-hearted stranger with the eyes of a raven.
A fire of living ice burns through the bones.

The man says,
"The doorway to the stars
I can open
But you must follow me"
The price:
Smoke,
but no heat.
Ashes
but no fire.

Gaze into this smoking mirror!
Your point of attention will be lost,
But,
"I will show you where to find it."

The Watchtower

From the watchtower the sentry observed the armies assembling.
He cast his gaze down upon their bright bloody shirts.
He would watch while they fought.
It was in his name that they chanted their war oaths.
The name that was just a memory to him now.

Marcel Pallais of Nicaragua

Marcel!
You breathed life into ideas
making them come alive in your room.
The smell of Nicaraguan cigar smoke,
so crisp and delicious,
whetted my appetite for more,
more ideas,
discussion,
truths to unearth.
Remember how I said,
"There's no other side to genocide."
It was all so alive then.
To me,
you were the light of the revolution.

But,
they waited until you left the library.
You had books under your arm,
Killers.
Your life was taken by hoodlums,
for the sake of secrecy,
an oath those corrupt will someday be unable to keep.

The Chicago paper said, it was counter-revolutionaries
punishing your family
for supporting the coalition against Somoza.
Or was it, as one of your poets said
leftists who ordered your assassination
because you found out
as a good reporter
they had killed Padre Jose Commodore?

Sometimes I wish I knew who it really was,
other times I'm glad I don't.

But I do promise you this,
I will travel someday to your country
and place flowers on your tomb.

I will glance about the cemetery
at the graves of the other martyrs
and then retire to a nearby cafe to engage
in what they tell me
is the national pastime of you Nicaraguans,
writing poetry.

I imgaine I will write a poem
about an old woman I have seen in Managua,
una Olividada* who remembers your face.
Yours was not a kindness
confined to ideology, race, or nation-state.
It was born from an innocent, thirsting, curiosity.
For you reached the high foundation.
Your friendship bridged the gap
between the first and third worlds.
The man God loved more than most mortals
carried, lodged in his heart,
a sacred flame.

Even as you rest you know
another day's bright sun will rise,
a new generation of idealists will emerge
to remind us of the best Nicaragua can offer.

*the forgotten one

Ode to the New Year: The Sacrifice of the Scapegoat

"Let us slay him, and see if his dreams live."
(*Epitaph from the tomb of Martin Luther King, Jr.*)

During the dark of the moon,
Toltec priests,
in the service of feathered snakes,
sacrificed a scapegoat,
slitting his throat with a flint-knife.

On the last of the dead days
the death maiden, Coatlicue,
drank the blood offering with ravenous lips.
The earth,
hearing the braying,
soaked up the sound like a sponge.

On the first night of the born-again year
the new moon rose only a little
above the cleft of the earth.

The next night,
the horn of the moon
was bathed in an orange, conjugal, light.

Of the scapegoat it can be said:
for those of us living on this earth
(and not the planet of the priests,
who make their prayers from the earth's higher double),
the offering of blood does not mean,
feeding human hearts to the god,
Quetzacoatl relegated to such a diet,
when an animal-god has donated his,
as offering,
a symbolic replacement.

The morning bird bids farewell
calling from the perches of grace,
a glorious star,
Venus in eclipse behind the sun,
the eye of the god
closing.

The historical man gave the sun a great gift:
pure substance itself,
an eagle
capturing the heart-star,
drinking directly from the light.
In the state of union,
another gift, the name, Quetzalcoatl.

On its return,
the bird will bring back
a snake
clenched in its beak.

On the eve of the new year,
when the sun shows us
its renewed radiance
I am reminded,
a heartbeat pulses,
glowing in the clay.
Fire-fibers flow
through the viscous veins
of the life-force.

I thank the scapegoat.
Once again, he has saved us from folly.

An Aztec Reflection

The lake flower of Tezcoco,
the white water lily,
is a kiss.

The sky sheds teardrops of turquoise.

I heard a man in the mountains say
they watched the eagle hatch from a safe place.

my canoe sails smoothly through beds of lake flowers

Women appear in the gleam of an eye
a hint of emerald luxuriousness,
a Venusian gleam,
an evening star at twilight.

green hummingbirds gather like honeybees to sip

I have drunk from the spring water of Chapultepec,
gazing at Smoking Man and Sleeping Woman,
the snows of summer upon them.

The old miner said he found a cave full of jade.

I died to the person I was
to offer my heart to the sun.

The flower wars are the illusion.

I overheard these words and phrases
when I listened to my heart's secret conversation.

The Lake Snake

In a dream,
a white female snake,
ten feet long
raised up on its coil,
stares closely at me
moving its head with huge brown eyes
slowly
    from side
      to side.
I would swear her name is Cleo,
and yes I am afraid,
    but only a little.
What does she see on such close inspection?
    a tangle of cloth woven at interesting places?
    a luminous egg with cracked fissures in the shell?

She thrusts her sinuous long body at me.
I feel her head softly punch the side of my skull.
Like a gummy fist
    bouncing
      off a hard surface,
my body becomes soft
    and seeps into
      the surrounding
        bright green water.

Blood Lightning

I feel heat lightning stirring in my blood.

In the pregnant desert badlands
ringing a river valley
living on the largesse
of mountains loved by clouds
magnetic currents constantly jump the track.

In my forearms I feel a soothing scratch.
The electricity of the blood burns.
An occasion for hot palms uplifted
and the crackling of first raindrops on the ground.

This case of blood lightning is discussed in Mayan circles.
They remember the hot spots in the body
and their activation sequence, solar and lunar.
Glowing hands my beseech the Goddess in service
or impart the healing fire coiling through the blood.

In my blood the mirror of a mountain lake
shows on its face the Lady with the Serpent Hair.
Writhing luminously, they charge the cold lake water.
Illumined streaks fracture its placidity.

I feel hot tracks smoking.
The clouds deliver silver flashes.
Remember the way the light waved in the water?
That was when it poured.

Huitzilopochtli

A spotted tiger implacably stalks
a bevy of geese under a moonlit sky.
Their downy feathers glisten silver
as they skirt the edge of a gleaming pond.
The geese paddle,
without fear,
towards the shore
hoping to escape into the friendly water.

The tiger anticipates their ploy.
He intercepts their retreat
herding them back towards a ridge
with threats from his paws.

A man is walking through pines
halfway up the hill.
The tiger has forgotten the geese.
A more interesting game awaits him.
Tigers can climb.

The man breaks, running,
towards a tree far from the flock.
He leaps into the boughs

The man is clinging to thin branches
in the tree's middle fork.
The tiger claws his way up the outside limbs.
The man kicks the tough wood.
It shudders.
The weight of the cat is too much.
He falls back to the ground,
his claws leaving long scratches.

His mate arrives.
The two box the swinging boughs.

The geese flee
and watch from the protection of the water.

The tigers continue to pummel
the limbs with their paws.
None of them snap.

Tiring of the game,
they leave the strange man
to his arboresque bivouac.

Hearing the geese begin to clack,
he gazes towards the pond.
White shadows glide over the water.

Hummingbird

the life current connecting all things
sounds like a hummingbird
swimming in air uncoiling

my heart beats as fast
as tiny wings

breathing mercuric air
silver seas lap on silk-embroidered senses

the intensity of touching woven shapes
jangle-fire frequency
signal electric tingles
up the spine bursting
like shooting stars
in the heart's deep cavity

Arise there, hummingbird!
heaven has given you flowers to suckle

The Rainbow Serpent

There is a white sun in the center of the soul,
a morning star submerging in the dawn,
an evening star soaring above the sunset.

Men have thought blood contains it,
in a luminous humor freed from enchainment of the body,
jagged hearts expiring on sacrificial stones.

All races are of one blood!
Antediluvian pulses throb in our veins,
drums pounding in our inner ears.

Eagles cry from their eyries
when the upswelling urge
disgorges the sound from their throats.

Snakes will crowd the earth shrines
in coiled throngs
when divine fire is released.

Golden flowers blossom
as plumes of light
swirl convergently at the hub.

And the spilt blood of a lamb
reminds us that sacrifice
is symbolic.

The morning star does not flame brighter
because of our bequest of blood.
The evening star does not darken due
to the advent of our deaths.

There is, only, a white star shining.

In the interior of all things, it blazes.
Its signature is the golden mean,
the spiral curl of spirit.

Light white clouds,
burnished by the wind,
kiss the earth.

And when the lamp of heaven
inflames the violet skein of water
a rainbow serpent rises
enjoining us with the light from its single eye.

The Seven Cities

They say a Spaniard named Coronado was
actually looking for Seven Cities of Cibola.
That he found seven Zuni villages
and no gold
dissuaded him.

He didn't look hard enough.

The doorway guarded by snakes
allows entry to the spiral staircase.

Gold is the color of life
when the heart breathes a calm fire.
Coronado was fooled by appearance,
and failed to find the inner element,
the touchstone
with which the wise communicate.

Seven cities,
seas,
mountains,
caves,
villages,
valleys,
power-points in the body,
musical notes,
reflect an intrinsic design
the compass pointing
to landmarks denoting
the next level of geography
on the map describing
the way home.

I and Thou

I love to listen to you
when your ear
touches the ground.
Whose footsteps are coming?

If your eyes fill with tears,
Are you happy for us?

I answer from the cave,
where the light is dim
shadows flicker on the walls in firelight,
and the creatures wear webbed feet.

The twins* have been here,
they gathered the brightest.
I was the one who agreed to return.

You and I listen
to the pulsing of earth veins,
and gaze into mirrors of smoky quartz.
We hear a beat skipping.
We see rose glimmer
growing in the rock.

Whose footsteps are coming?
It is another who posits,
"I and Thou."

*Zuni

46

The Water-Jug

(after a description by Frank Waters in the Book of the Hopi)

Kneel in front of the ocean's blue lips.
Place your prayer feather there.
Take pinches of cornmeal
and draw a line in the direction of the people.
Into the water-jug put
a sprig of seaweed,
a small seashell,
water dogs that you will dig up with your eagle feather,
and some sand from the ocean bottom.
Lastly, add salt water.

I travelled far on my migration
to reach the western ocean,
through burning deserts,
where hot sand scorched my feet.
Masaw* was very explicit,
blunt never rude.
A young unmarried man of perfect character must make the journey.

With this water-jug-
fresh water will pour from the jar,
salt will collect at the bottom.

Later races have wondered
why my people have lived in such
inhospitable places.
They do not know,
Masaw wished it so.

*The Great Spirit (Hopi word)

The Blessing Way

Standing on the velvet-blue slopes
of the Lukachukai mountains,
the Colorado plateau stretches,
a wrinkled skin,
over the face of the land.
The eyes of the people are open.
Moonglow arms embrace the sunset.

Light pours in through the smoke hole
of the larger hogan, and illuminates
the mesa-rifts, huge splotched spines of orange,
winding sculpted channels painted
on the canvas of the dance.
In this open-roofed hogan,
                       we walk.
We chant the blessing way,
sprinkle pollen to each side,
the path glistening white,
or amber-red
when Father's sun banner is raised.

Winter chill quickens the pine tree sap.
Furry cones blossom centripetal star-points.

There is a moment,
as the full moon rises in the west,
and the sun sets in the east,
that the two,
            counterpoised,
                 fuse.

Look!
What are the hell-holes of the uranium mines compared to this!
Fleas arguing over who owns the dog.
I own none of these gifts,
only,
a pair of moccasins who love the path.

I walk to the mountain-top.
The sun and moon exchange wedding vows.
On their ring fingers,
I kiss them.

On wings that cast carven shadows on the earth,
I am pulled through the smoke hole.
I let the light lift me, lift me
until I taste the sweet spring water
flowing from the breast of the green meadow.

The Big Man *(for Grandfather David)*

It is said by the elders
that the husband of mother earth
walks the land,
even flys above the trees.
Remember the vision I told you about;
my body buzzing
bees congregating in the heart's honeycomb,
issuing, enmasse, from the mouth of the cave.

Rising towards the skylight,
I see a big man.
His face is fierce,
yet I'm not afraid of him,
Shoulder-length black-hair,
long arms hang at his sides.
He stares down at me, curious perhaps.

You said your grandfather had seen him too,
one evening outside the front windows of your pueblo home.
I asked, "When did this happen?" you said, "1915."

Then you gave me the Matthiessen book,
people at Wounded Knee reported seeing him
walking down by the river during the FBI siege.

When we went to visit Grandfather David at Hopi
he said, "the big man?"

"He doesn't let me go to bed.
He tugs on my toes when I try to sleep.
We walk through sides there are
white men and women laughing at us
and Indian people too.

We fly over the mountain.
The tree of life stands in the sun.
Stacked corn sheaves lie around it.
A shepherd's crook and planting stick
lean against the wood of the tree."

Masaw implores me, "Please take these!"
"Remind mankind: Do not forget my spiritual gifts!"

When we camp that night at Prophecy Rock
in our sleeping bags on open ground,
breathing easily, we feel clouds condense near us.

The first rain is soft, female.
and then later, it pours down
hard, driving.

We move, quickly, under metal roofs
over roadside picnic tables.
We hear the rain pound on the cover slats.
I marvel . . . our vision is true!

Your dream was of a woman
standing next to a picnic table.
When you met her later in person
she, too, had seen the big man.

The morning sun breaks over the spine of first mesa.
Red mud lays thick on the ground.
We walk over to the petroglyphs.
The Great Spirit holds the crook and planting stick.

Sitting on a rock you hear a coyote call.
I am staring at the wet red clay,
the face of the light, bright upon it.

A couple of weeks later
you called to tell me
you found the shepherd's staff,
a curved cactus cane, you said.
the rod of a century plant,
laying on a roadside picnic table downstate.
You phoned around to see whose it was.

I remember the Great Spirit saying somewhere,
probably in the Book of Hopi,
"all you need is my planting stick, to live here as I do."

I have been planting corn.
I plan to plant it always.

The Earth's Bright Mantle

Walking on the solemn earth
along the golden rib of the mesa
are the desert flowers,
after the first rain,
stitched together,
glistening,
like beads of dawn dew strung on a silver chain
by an adept spider sewing
the weaves of the web.

When breath exhales upon them in prayer
secret spirals spring upward
and more tiny pearls join the glowing chain
ascending towards the mouth of praise.

All these things have come to be
in reverence and praise
for the genius within nature
because with a nighthawk's eyes
a human being sees the earth
wearing
a robe of starlight.

Santa Clara Canyon *(for Jose Lucero)*

The day began hot.

Summer's fire baked
the spittle from the mesas and

denuded every leaf on each cottonwood tree
of its silver chain of moisture. It was a day
to find a way to heal suffering bodies, afflicted

with poisons that stripped green bushes and trees from
along the riverbanks of blood that flowed through courses
no longer spiral, but made straight by the hand of man. The
highway through the valley was hot enough to make of the Jemez
mountains a mirage behind a veil of mist. The tough pinon trees were

the only ones holding so firm under the burning sun. Their nuts were growing,
budding curlicue's of shell intimating a wisdom the trees have always known.
Almost imperceptibly, within the space of a hundred yards or so, the brave
pinons gave way to stately cedars and spruces, as the altitude moved restlessly
from the zone of the baked desert mesas, phasing into the alpine. The spruces
were much taller, their roots less deep, however. As the road curved down into
the final approach to the canyon an unmistakable sound floated through the
oceans of smell such chords associate themselves with throughout their

lives. Where the pinon is piquant, and only stringent because of salt,
its melody is played on a bass drum. With the spruce a violin with its
long bow would play a gentle music on branches extended from the neck,
playing find needles on each string. The sound flowing through the
stalks of grass, and rhyming inside the heart-wood of the trees, adding
more circles every year, making even the callow crags shiver; the
whistled piping of the flute! Gay fingers press on air holes that emit
sound. The sound springs from the musical earth. It smells like
baby's breath. Water. The stream is singing in a melodious warbling
voice. Its spirit is free. It sings through each bend. It whistles
through every curve. The Santa Clara is a swift moving artery, pumping
earth's life blood through vessels which carry more than blood. The canyon
is narrow towards the bottom. The road brushes near the canyon

walls. No sun has yet penetrated. The mist hovers above, protective.
At every curve a flute octave rings. A human spine at such times needs
to be harmonium whose vertebrae become tuning forks, the spinal cord;
a harp being plucked. Or rather, the vertebrae are no longer locks,
which stop the flow of healing water. They are whirlpools, which
instead of sucking energy in, swirl it out. Poisons will then leave the
body, and it will be open to the impregnation of spirit in all its
material guises. Mushrooms are growing alongside the road, tucked into

the folds of grass in wet, pregnant, spots. It is as if they sprout from
blood seeds where the Great Mother has menstruated. Mushrooms do bear the
crown of creation, and flecks of placenta mark the bells. The mushrooms
call. They blaze with luminosity. They darken in the shade. Up ahead,
the glistening stream winds like a white snake through trees arranged like

the columns of temples set free, passing under the front porticoes, the
doors to the holy of holies, open. A moment passes. The Great Spirit
doesn't burst through the clouds hurling lightning bolts. The green grass

along the track is much greener. It ripples as if someone were petting
the fur of a cat. The ponds of Santa Clara appear, draped like opals

around a maiden's neck. Indians and tourists are fishing for trout.

Their lines droop lazily into the water. Meadows open, vast shining crops of green hair tousled by light breezes. Aspen trees like white candles

burning flare along the ridges of the mountain tops. Fists of granite jut from the higher foliage. At the fourth pond a bridge spans the earthen dam. A crossing over into the forest. The trail ends abruptly.

Invisible feet tread softly on the forest floor. Rotting logs are strewn everywhere. The ground exudes the unmistakable scent of decay. Mushrooms and flowers pop up at every step. A five-pointed lavender flower is lit up by the sun as it parts the clouds. The sky begins to clear. The trees drip water and the droplets split the light into ringing sevens, flute

key-covers popping up like ground hogs poking their noses out at the smell of spring. A head is pushing against mother's membrane. A shuddering echoes from the crags. A blue baby is being born. The ground is soaked with blood. Deer lick the baby clean. A raccoon cuts the umbilical cord with a flint knife. A shaman-bear teaches the foundling to walk. An eagle's wings flap inside its heart. An eagle swoops down. The dwarf breaks the shell of its egg, stretching its wings and flying. In its forehead, the wings spread. The claws clutch at the brain stem. The

crags beckon. Whoosh. Feathers tip-toe on the tree tops. Aspen leaves fan its face. Light warms its belly. Cool water from springs high on the mountain quenches a thirsty throat. The water spins like a wheel. transparent gears, notched in light, turn effortlessly. Rocks cool the spring when it jumps from one pool to another. Slivers of silt wash against the banks of a microscopic shore. The water stays clean inside the undulation, but becomes dirty when the motion reverses itself. Bacteria, slime, algae grow along the side, cutting the amount of light into the water. Fungus crawls on all fours over the forest floor. It attacks dying logs. Dead bodies fall back to earth. The springs give birth to a baby whose light body is whirling with eddies. Earth stomach pushes the baby through the blood sack, and though its face may be smeared, it sucks for water, cool clean water that washes the old blood away, and nourishes new blood, ground on a lapidary wheel of light. Awakening at the spring two eyes stare out at the world. The aspen trees sing praises of healing land and healing water. The bear cave looms like a yawning abyss from across the valley below. Their scent sends shock waves through the senses. A decision is made. To descend on foot upwind of the cave. Today is not the day for visiting the master. It is not about his death, or the death of the visitor to his cave. He doesn't expect a pupil to return. If a student did, the lesson was not learned.

Such disrespect would mean death. Cradled near the cave on the downslope is a fold of land back up against a hill where a grove of aspens stand. A sacred encampment awaits. Encoded in cells of tissue in the human body and in nature are junction spots where the worlds meet, where the light body touches the holy organs of spirit. It is then that the trees speak,

saying, "Welcome back!" The valley lifts up her skirt and lets her creatures place their heads on the soft down of her vaginal hair. Smell deeply! Remember you have been here before. And the rock, where the

shamans performed their marriage rites is standing where it is supposed to be, right in the center of the grove, the only rock. It is taller than a

man, wider. Its memory is as old as the place. It remembers that when

shamans danced they flew into the underworld with their bodies. It
remembers when sounds could move mountains, and move the sacred stones in

their present places. When warriors camped here, the ceremonies
made, the prayer sticks charged, before the hunts, sanctified the
spirits of the animals, and they let themselves be taken. A hand has

touched the rock. Life overlaps again. The hand floats in a sea of
love. Return again, kind one! A trail of lavender flowers, the ones
seen on the beginning of the journey, the plant allies of the vision,
appear again to lead the spirit-body out through a sea of green diaphanous
liquidity. A verdure skein floats, gently rocking. Everything is so

still. A momentary stab of fear prickles down the spine. The ebb and
flow of union or separation, as motion swirls in the spine, either
centripetally or centrifugally, hinges on a confidence gained in trusting
the vision or the personal "I." Where is the flower? There! A finger
points. A shaft of sunlight, again, weaves through the trees
illuminating a five-pointed island in the sea of tranquility. Those
flowers are spirit emblems marking signposts of confidence to the new
seer. The trail leads right down to the fourth pond. It glistens

beneath a pavillion of trees. There are untold mansions in every water
droplet. Light pours in all the rooms. The tree tops arch into the
sky forming a fluted vault. White clouds dance on the mountain tops. The
sun shoots arrows piercing transparent skin. The water gurgles. Drink!
Drink! Cool soft caresses gently wash over new bodies. The sun plays
guitar on the strings of the tree branches. Water accompanies on flute.
Naked beings of light, water, blood, and breath sit growing warm on rocks
in the stream. Cool shade filters over the light as the day grows long.
The night is coming. The night is like water when it spins, it makes the
water move faster. The grains of blood ground this day will shine
phosphorescently in the dark. The darkness defines their globular shape
as they grow into silver veins wending their way through the mountains of
the world. The night hangs glowing chandeliers on the roof of the sky.

The night lights candles in fireflies and kindles earthglow in all
living things. Each creature wears a robe woven with light.
Facing the dark a being knows a mother lode is carried
in its breast. Roses bloom from the heart's blood.
For each thing has its own cocoon, spun
with silvan flax. Where the light
shell breaks, a being of blood
is born from a devic uterus.

It keeps its butterfly wings of light
even as it lives in the world.
And water, sweet water
washes over both the
light and blood

until both spin according
to its harmony in
a spiral motion

ever moving towards a
transparent

center.

A Poet Writing His Requiem

I have lived a long time already,
And tasted your enchantments.
With the blessing of the Muse I have found favour,
those holy things departing which mortals savour.

I shall not cry with the passing of the chorus,
Whose lofty music bends down the soul,
For its weight held me to the hallowed earth,
And the harp player plucking allowed the god his mirth.

Into a farther field will the days retreat,
And I will rest in its pasture by the brook.
For the sweet gurgling water reminds me of our mother,
She who with her soft deathly hands my life will smother.

It is then my breath will fly most fleetingly,
Like the rustling of the wind over the cottonwood trees.
The spirit of the river, too, shall bid me goodbye,
Even as I lay down beside her to let my life lie.

And again as the dust settles o'er my corpse,
I will shed each suit of clothes as I go.
Until the hallowed earth holds me no more,
I will again be a seed on the shelf in her store.